The Birth of Jesus

of

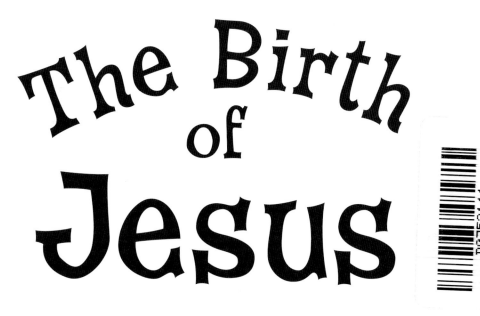

and other Bible Stories

Retold by Vic Parker

Miles
Kelly

First published in 2011 by Miles Kelly Publishing Ltd
Harding's Barn, Bardfield End Green, Thaxted, Essex, CM6 3PX, UK

2 4 6 8 10 9 7 5 3 1

EDITORIAL DIRECTOR *Belinda Gallagher*
ART DIRECTOR *Jo Cowan*
EDITOR *Carly Blake*
DESIGNERS *Michelle Cannatella, Joe Jones*
JUNIOR DESIGNER *Kayleigh Allen*
COVER DESIGNER *Joe Jones*
CONSULTANT *Janet Dyson*
PRODUCTION MANAGER *Elizabeth Collins*
REPROGRAPHICS *Stephan Davis, Ian Paulyn*

ISBN 978-1-84810-399-3

Printed in China

British Library Cataloguing-in-Publication Data
A catalogue record for this book is available from the British Library

ACKNOWLEDGEMENTS
The publishers would like to thank the following artists
who have contributed to this book:

The Bright Agency Katriona Chapman, Dan Crisp (inc. cover),
Giuliano Ferri, Mélanie Florian

Advocate Art Andy Catling, Alida Massari

*The publishers would like to thank Robert Willoughby and
the London School of Theology for their help in compiling this book.*

Made with paper from a sustainable forest

www.mileskelly.net   info@mileskelly.net
www.factsforprojects.com

Self-publish your
children's book

buddingpress.co.uk

Contents

The Birth of Jesus

In the town of Nazareth lived a woman called Mary, who was engaged to marry a young man called Joseph, a local carpenter. When she told Joseph she was expecting a baby he was very upset. The baby couldn't be his because they weren't married. And in those days, if a single woman was expecting a baby it was quite shameful. However, Joseph had a dream in which an angel told him, "Don't be afraid to take Mary as your wife. Her baby is the Son of God Himself. The prophets of long ago foretold that He would come and save everyone from their sins. Raise Him as your own son. God wants you to call Him Jesus." After this Joseph felt much better. He realized he would be honoured to bring the little boy up as his own, and he and Mary married straight away.

However, near the time that the baby was to be born, another problem arose. The emperor Augustus Caesar ordered a survey of all the people in his lands. He commanded that every man had to travel to where he was born, taking his family with him to have their names put on a register. Joseph had been born in the city of Bethlehem in Judea, in southern Israel, which was quite a distance from the village of Nazareth. Mary was heavily pregnant and travelling would be very difficult for her. Nevertheless, the couple did not have a choice. They packed what they would need for the trip and set off. Mary couldn't possibly walk all that way, so she rode on a donkey. It was a bumpy and tiring journey for a woman so close to having a baby.

By the time the couple reached Bethlehem they were exhausted, hungry and dusty. Joseph began trying to find a room in which they could stay. He trudged with the donkey and Mary from one lodging place to the next. But to the couple's dismay, everywhere was full. The city was bustling with travellers who had come to register for the emperor's survey.

As they were turned away from one place after another, Mary began to feel that the baby was on its way. Hurriedly, Joseph banged on the door of the nearest inn. After a few moments, the busy innkeeper peered outside. "Don't bother asking, we're full," he said, as soon as he saw the travellers.

"Wait, please help us!" cried Joseph, stopping the innkeeper from shutting the door on them. "My wife's about to have a baby. She can't give birth out here in the street! Haven't you got a spare corner somewhere you could squeeze us in?"

"Well…" said the innkeeper, looking at poor Mary in pain on the donkey. "I haven't got a single room to spare, but you're welcome to shelter in my stable if you don't mind the animals."

"Thank you, thank you so much," Joseph said, gratefully shaking the man's hand, and the innkeeper showed them the way to his stable.

It was there, with the donkeys, oxen and sheep looking on, that Mary gave birth to the baby boy who was to be the saviour of the world. She wrapped Him up in cloths and nestled Him in a manger full of straw.

And baby Jesus was warm and safe, with His mother and foster father by His side.

Matthew chapter 1; Luke chapter 2

9

The Shepherds' Visit

On the night that Jesus was born, the city of Bethlehem throbbed with people, while the surrounding countryside was peaceful except for a few shepherds and their flocks. The shepherds were taking turns at sleeping and watching. They made sure that the sheep weren't wandering away and kept watch for hungry wolves.

All at once the starry night sky above the shepherds blazed as bright as day. Then it blazed brighter still, too bright for the shepherds to look up. They shielded their eyes from the blinding glare as an angel appeared high overhead. The shepherds were terrified.

"Don't be afraid," came the angel's voice, clear through the still, cold night. "I bring you wonderful news – wonderful news for everyone on Earth. This very night a child has been born who will be the saviour of all people. You can find Him in a stable in Bethlehem, lying in a manger."

The air was filled with singing more beautiful than the shepherds had ever heard, as hundreds of thousands of angels suddenly appeared in the heavens. "Glory to God,"

they sang. "And peace to all people
on Earth."

The shepherds stood
transfixed until the angels had
finished their song. Then the heavenly
music died and the angels faded away.
Could it really be true the shepherds
wondered? In ancient stories prophets
had predicted for hundreds of years
that a man would come who
would save everyone from their
sins. They called him the Messiah.
Maybe he had really come at last.

The shepherds hurried off
to Bethlehem, to see for
themselves. They searched
through the streets until they heard
the sound of a newborn baby crying

from a stable behind an inn. There they found Mary and Joseph looking after baby Jesus. In great excitement, they told the startled couple all that they had seen and heard. Mary fell very quiet, taking it all in.

The shepherds stayed for a while, marvelling at the baby boy who they had been told was the Messiah, but they had to return to their flocks. All the way back they couldn't stop talking about the amazing chorus of angels and how their words had come true. They told everyone they met, praising God and giving thanks for all that they had seen and been told.

Luke chapter 2

Follow the Star

Far away in distant lands to the east, there lived some wise men who were astrologers. Every night they gazed up at the sky and studied the stars, trying to work out what their movements around the heavens meant for people on Earth. One night they were stunned by a brand new star that appeared much bigger and brighter than the rest. They hurried to consult their ancient books to see what it could mean. The wise men became very excited by what they found, and were in no doubt that a great Jewish prophecy had come true. The star was a sign that a baby had been born who would become the king of God's Chosen People. The wise men decided to set off to find him at once. They loaded up their camels with supplies and set off into the desert, heading in the direction of the star that blazed each night in the sky. Finally, they arrived in the city of Jerusalem.

News soon reached King Herod of Judea that strangers from the east had arrived in Jerusalem. These strangers were searching for a newborn baby they were calling the 'King of the Jews'. Of course Herod didn't like the sound of that at all. As far as he was concerned he had been crowned King of the Jews and he wanted it to stay that way. He certainly wasn't going to put up with rumours spreading about a rival – who fulfilled one of the ancient prophecies no less. It would just stir up trouble among the people and they might rise up against him.

King Herod set about dealing with the problem in his cold, calculated way. First, he called a meeting of all the chief Jewish religious leaders to find out more. "Where do your ancient books say the Messiah is to be born?" he asked, innocently.

"In Bethlehem," the holy men answered.

Then King Herod called his guards and

ordered them to find the wise men and bring them to him. "But do it in secret," he commanded. "I don't want people to get the impression that I think these men and their rumours are important."

The wise men were nervous when they were summoned to see the king. They had heard that Herod could be a cruel leader. However, they were surprised to find him most polite, interested and even helpful in their quest. "The Jewish elders have told me that you shouldn't be looking in Jerusalem," he explained. "Try Bethlehem instead. When you have found the future king, do come back and tell me all about it. I'd like to go and pay my respects too."

The wise men had no idea that King Herod only wanted to know where the baby was so he could have him killed. They set off to Bethlehem and followed the star to where it appeared to hang biggest

and brightest in the sky, over the house in which Mary and Joseph were now staying. The wise men were surprised to find the baby in an ordinary home rather than a splendid palace. They bowed to worship Him and presented Mary and Joseph with gifts – jewelled gold caskets, and the rare spices frankincense and myrrh.

Herod never got to hear of the wise men's success. The night before they were due to set off home, they had a troubling dream that warned them not to return to the king. The wise men took a different route back to their lands in the east and Herod never found them.

Matthew chapter 2

Flight from Danger

After the wise men had visited Jesus, an angel appeared to Joseph in a dream. "Herod is trying to find the baby to kill Him," the angel warned. "Take Him and Mary to Egypt. It will be a long, hard journey, but it will take you safely out of the cruel king's reach. Stay there until I tell you it is safe to return."

Joseph woke up with a start. He woke Mary and told her to make ready to travel straight away. The family hurried through the dark, sleeping streets of Bethlehem and onto the road to Egypt.

Meanwhile back in Jerusalem, Herod was waiting for the wise men to return from Bethlehem and tell him where the baby king of kings was. He waited… and waited… Eventually he realized that the wise men weren't coming – he had been tricked! Herod flew into a fury and roared at his army chief, "Send your men to search every house in Bethlehem. I want every boy under two years of age put to death immediately!"

By the time the soldiers arrived in Bethlehem to carry out their terrible task, Jesus, Mary and Joseph were miles away in Egypt. They stayed there for several months until an angel appeared to Joseph once more, telling him that King Herod had died and it was safe to go back to Israel.

However Joseph did not take his family back to Bethlehem. The city was far too close to Jerusalem, where King Herod's son was now on the throne. Instead, he travelled north back to their home in the sleepy town of Nazareth in the remote area of Galilee.

Matthew chapter 2

Jesus in the Temple

Every year at the festival of Passover, all Jewish men went to visit the temple in Jerusalem to pray and give thanks to God. Joseph always went and, like many women, Mary went too. Of course the number of people who crowded into the city was huge. The lodging houses were heaving, people packed streets and the temple itself was totally crammed. Like many parents with young children, Mary and Joseph left Jesus with a relative or neighbour when they went to celebrate the festival. But when He reached the age of twelve, they decided Jesus was old enough to go with them.

The family travelled to Jerusalem with a large group of relatives and friends. When the festival was over, they all set off to travel home. Joseph walked with the men, Mary chatted to the women and Jesus ran back and forth with the other children.

But at the end of the first day's journey, when the group of travellers began to make camp for the night, Jesus had disappeared. Mary and Joseph called for their son at the tops of their voices, but He didn't come. With a rising sense of panic, the couple dashed up and down, describing Jesus to everyone and asking if anyone had seen Him. No one had. Darkness was drawing in fast. "There's nothing else we can do tonight, but as soon as it gets light tomorrow we'll retrace our steps and find Him," Joseph comforted his weeping wife.

Of course, Mary and Joseph didn't sleep for worrying about where Jesus was and whether He was safe. At sunrise Mary and Joseph began making their way back to Jerusalem, asking everyone they met if they had seen a lost twelve-year-old boy. They reached the city and hunted around its bustling streets for two days, but there was no sign of Him.

The third day came and in desperation Mary and Joseph went to look in the great temple itself. To their astonishment, there they found Jesus deep in discussion with a group of Jewish priests and leaders.

"Your son has such a wise understanding of the ancient writings, we can't believe He is only twelve," the holy men told Mary

and Joseph. "He asks questions that most people never think to ask, and He's been giving us answers too!"

But Mary and Joseph just wanted to know what had happened to Jesus. "Where on earth have you been?" They cried. "We've been worried sick!"

Jesus replied calmly, "You should have known that you would find me in my Father's house."

Luke chapter 2

John the Baptist

Mary's sister Elizabeth and her husband Zachariah had a son called John, who grew up to be a holy man. John went to live on his own in the countryside of Judea, so he could think about God and pray without being distracted. He wore only a simple robe woven from camel hair and survived by eating locusts and wild honey.

When he was about thirty years old, he began preaching to anyone he came across. "Be sorry for your sins and turn away from evil," was his message, "so you can enter God's Kingdom, which is nearly here!"

John was such a powerful speaker that people travelled especially to see him. People from all walks of life flocked from towns, villages and the city of Jerusalem too. From poor common people, to powerful Jewish groups such as the Pharisees and the Sadducees, as well as farmers, shop keepers, tax collectors and even Roman soldiers. They usually found John on the banks of the River Jordan.

"What does God want from us?" they would ask.

John would advise, "Be kind and

generous. Treat each other fairly. Don't hurt anyone, neither in your actions nor words."

John's teachings were so stirring that people often asked him if he was the saviour – the Messiah spoken of in the ancient writings. "No," John would insist, "but I am trying to prepare the way for His coming."

One after the other, people would tell John all the things they had done wrong in their lives, hanging their heads in shame. They felt truly sorry for their sins and promised they wouldn't do them again, and that they would turn to God and try to live by His rules. Then John baptized them in the holy river. He dipped the people into the water and gave them God's blessing, so their sins were washed away and they could begin afresh. "I'm only baptizing you with water," John told them, "but the man who is coming will baptize you with the fire of the Holy Spirit. He is so holy that I am not even good enough to undo his sandals."

One day, among the crowd on the banks of the Jordan, Jesus was waiting to be baptized. John knew who He was immediately. "It's not right that I baptize you," John told Jesus. "You should be baptizing me."

But Jesus insisted that it was what God wanted. So together the men walked into the river. As soon as John had baptized Jesus, the clouds above them parted and light blazed down on Jesus. A dove came gliding down and hovered above Jesus, and John knew that it was God's Holy Spirit coming down to Him. Then a voice spoke into everyone's minds saying, "This is my beloved son, with whom I am very pleased."

Matthew chapter 3; Mark chapter 1; Luke chapter 3; John chapter 1

Jesus' First Miracle

Jesus went into the desert of Judea to pray for forty days and forty nights. Then He left the River Jordan and the desert lands of Judea in the south behind Him and went back to live in Galilee in the north. He knew God wanted Him to begin teaching everyone what they had to do to enter His Kingdom. Several followers of John the

Baptist went with Jesus to help.

Jesus preached in Jewish places of worship called synagogues. "Beg God to forgive your sins," He told everyone, just like John the Baptist had, "so you can enter the Kingdom of God, which is coming." News soon spread that Jesus was an exciting speaker and He quickly built a following.

Not long after Jesus had arrived back in Galilee, His mother Mary told Him that they had been invited to a wedding in Cana. It was to be a big event and the wedding celebrations were set to go on for several days.

Sitting down at the feast for the wedding, everyone was having a wonderful time. About halfway through, Mary noticed that the wine was starting to run out. She knew it would be highly embarrassing for the bride and bridegroom if they couldn't offer their guests any more to drink. So she whispered to Jesus, feeling sure that He could help.

"I'm sorry but I can't do anything about it," Jesus whispered back. "It's not a good time right now."

But Mary turned to the flustered servants and said, "I've noticed that you are low on wine, but my son can help. Do exactly what He says."

Jesus sighed. He gave His mother a gentle smile. Then He told the servants, "Fill all the empty wine jars up to the brim with water." They hurried to do as He said. "Now pour some into a goblet and take it to your boss, the steward, for tasting," Jesus

instructed. They did so, rather worried, but to their astonishment the steward smacked his lips, clapped his hands and ordered it to be served to the guests at once. The water had turned into wine. Not only that, but excellent wine – better than they had previously been serving. The steward strode straight over to the bridegroom to congratulate him on his good taste and generosity.

Through the power of God His Father, Jesus had performed His first miracle. There were many more to come.

Matthew chapter 4; Mark chapter 1; Luke chapter 4; John chapters 1, 2

Jesus Goes Fishing

Jesus sailed out on the Sea of Galilee in a boat belonging to two of His followers, Peter and Andrew, who were fishermen. "Throw your nets into the water. Let's see if there are any fish today," Jesus suggested.

"We already know there aren't," Peter replied gloomily. "We were fishing all last night and we didn't catch a thing."

"Well, why not try again?" Jesus urged.

"I don't think there's much point," Peter shrugged. Then he saw a strange gleam in Jesus' eyes. "But I suppose there's no harm in having another go."

He and Andrew lowered their nets and waited… Then after a while, the brothers went to lift them up again. To their astonishment, the nets were so heavy with fish that they couldn't raise them. The stunned pair had to signal for help from a nearby boat, belonging to the two sons of a man called Zebedee. Their names were James and John and they rowed over as quickly as they could to help.

Jesus watched the four men work hard together. It took all their strength to heave the enormous catch aboard. Soon Peter and Andrew's little boat was full of shiny, wriggling fish, and so weighed down in the water that it was in danger of sinking.

The men knew that this sort of catch was unheard of. Something miraculous must have happened. Peter fell on his knees before Jesus and said, "Lord, I'm not good enough to be one of your followers. I shouldn't have doubted what you said, I should have just done it straight away."

"Don't worry," Jesus said, kindly. "Anyway, I'm going to show you how to catch people instead of fish…"

From then on, Peter, Andrew, James and John stayed at Jesus' side and helped Him.

Matthew chapter 4; Mark chapter 1; Luke chapter 5